W9-BAQ-302

580L

PEACHTREE CITY LIBRARY
201 Willowbend Road
Peachtree, GA 30269

BLAST OFF TO EARTH!
A LOOK AT GEOGRAPHY

WRITTEN AND ILLUSTRATED BY

LOREEN LEEDY

HOLIDAY HOUSE   NEW YORK

Go home, Woofer!

Woof!

TO VICHI

Copyright © 1992 by Loreen Leedy

Printed in the United States of America

All rights reserved

First Edition

Library of Congress Cataloging-in-Publication Data
Leedy, Loreen.
    Blast-off to Earth! : a look at geography / Loreen Leedy. — 1st
ed.
        p.   cm.
    Summary: A group of aliens on a field trip visit each of the
continents on Earth and learn about some of their unique features.
    ISBN 0-8234-0973-2
    1. Geography—Juvenile literature.   [1. Geography.
2. Continents.]   I. Title.
G175.L44   1992   92-2567   CIP   AC
910—dc20

WELCOME
TO THE
MILKY WAY GALAXY

PLEASE FLY WITH CARE

How long till we get there, Mr. Quark?
Just a few more nanoseconds.
I have visual contact! It looks like a big, blue marble.
ROBOT WIRING

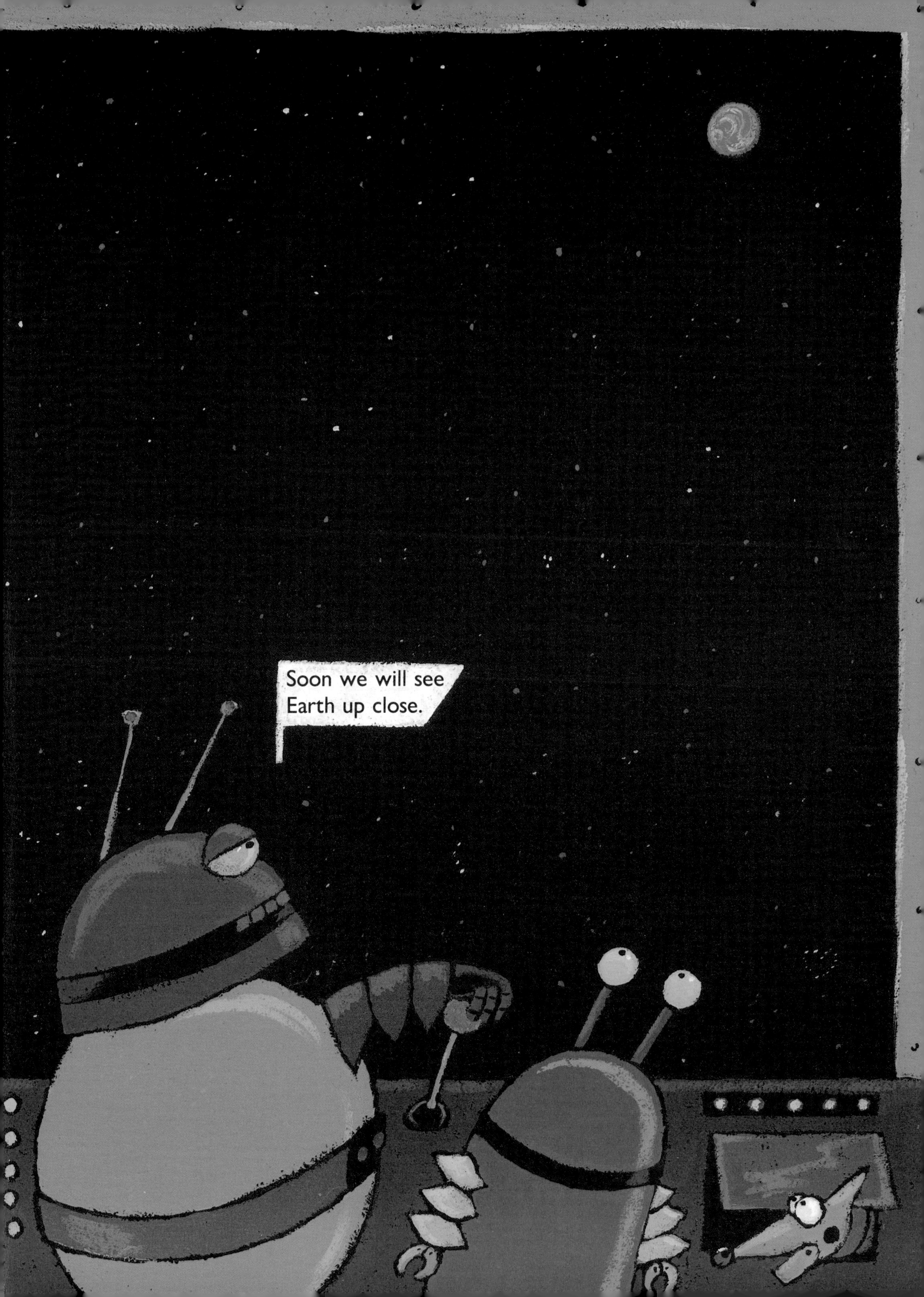
Soon we will see Earth up close.

Look at all that water!
The earth's surface is about 70% water and 30% land.
The large areas of water are oceans.
The large land masses are continents.

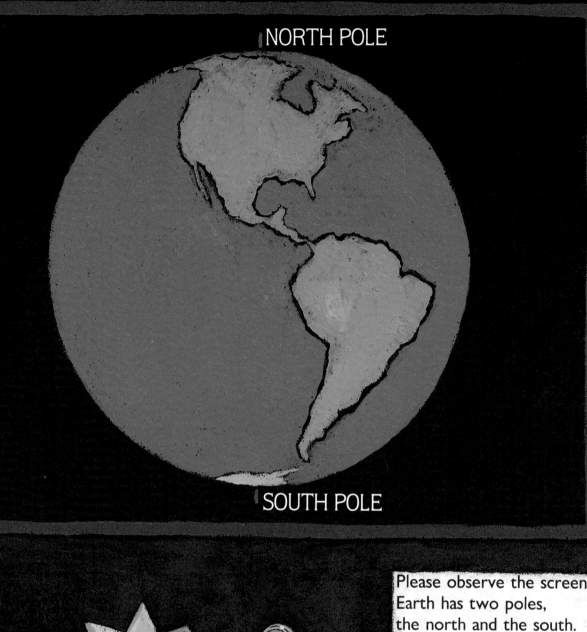

NORTH POLE

SOUTH POLE

Please observe the screen.
Earth has two poles,
the north and the south.
The climate is cold
near the poles.

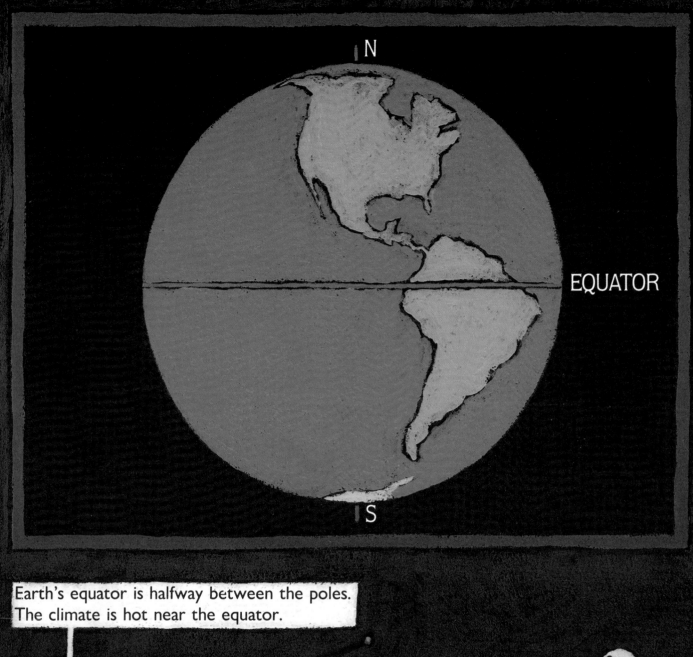

Earth's equator is halfway between the poles.
The climate is hot near the equator.

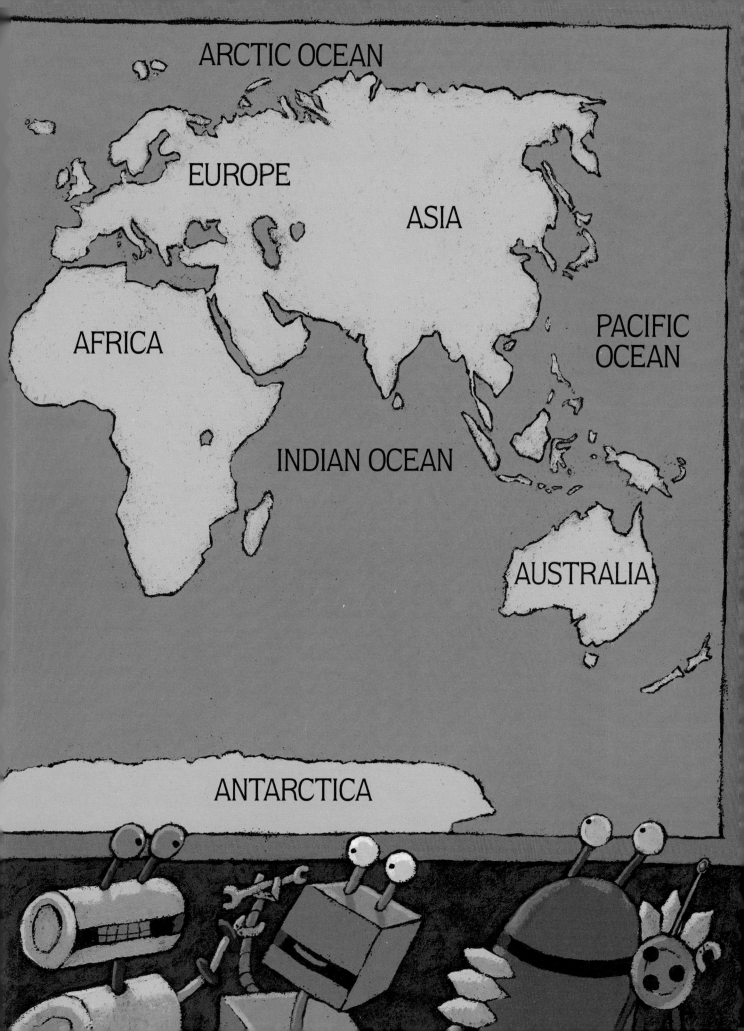

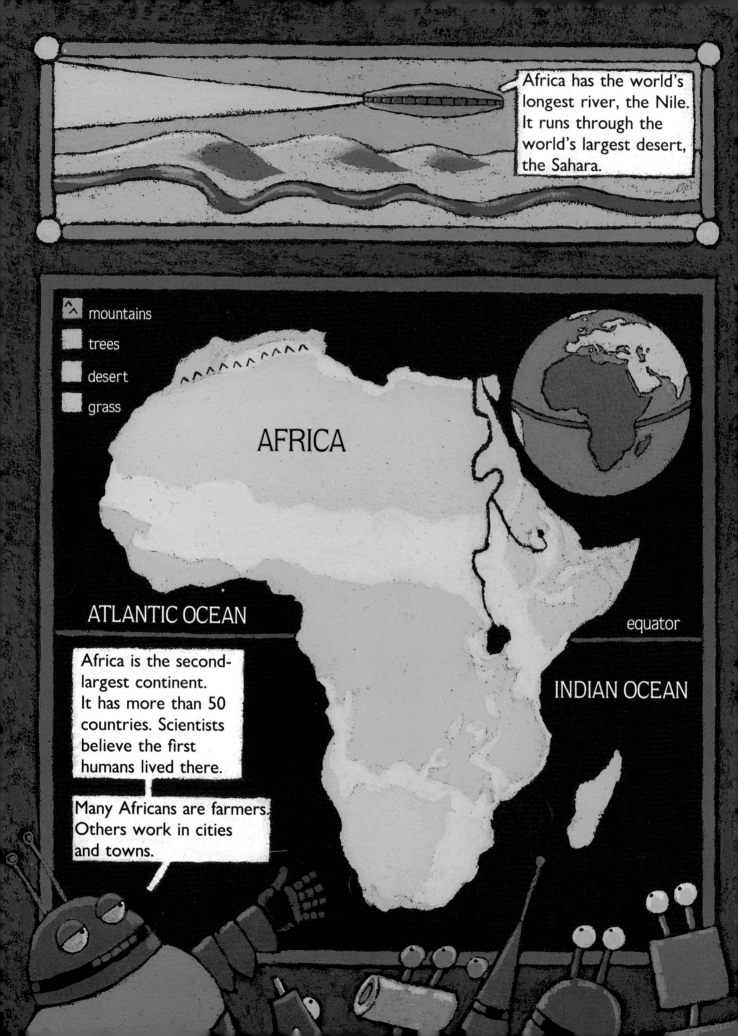

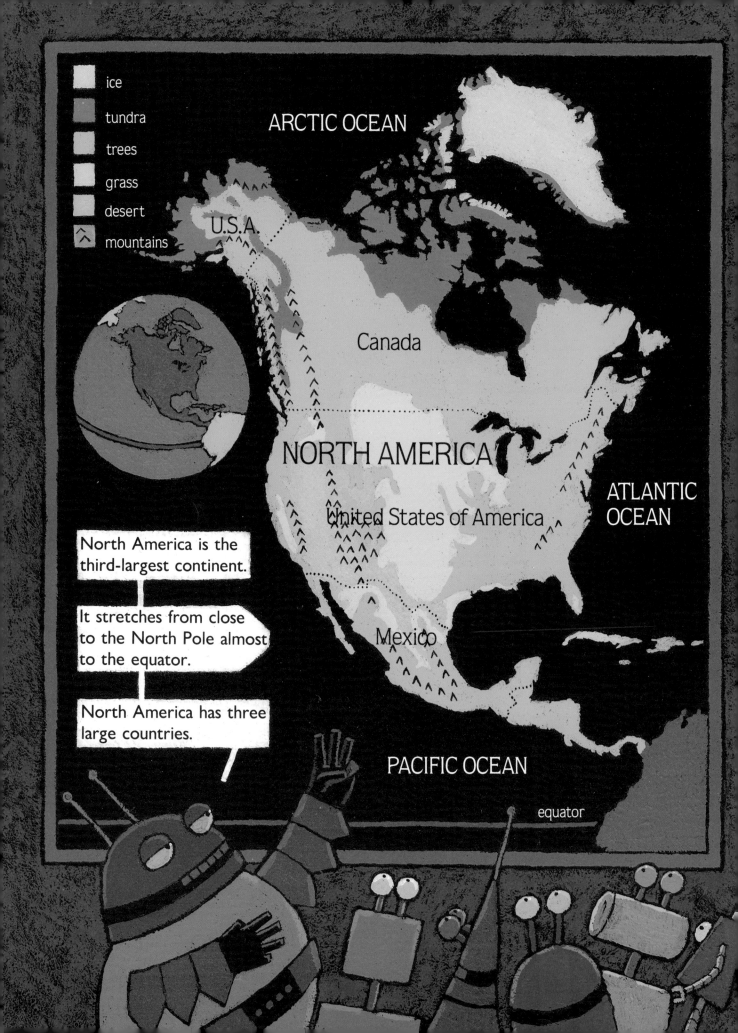

ATLANTIC OCEAN

ANTARCTICA

• South Pole

PACIFIC OCEAN

Antarctica is the fifth-
largest continent.
It is located at the
South Pole, and is
covered with ice.
The ice is over
a mile thick!

It is too cold for
humans to live there.

INDIAN OCEAN

Just like scientists and
explorers, we can
visit Antarctica.

All aboard! We are leaving Earth now!
Awwwwww! Do we have to, Mr. Quark?
Yes. But we can come back again on another field trip.

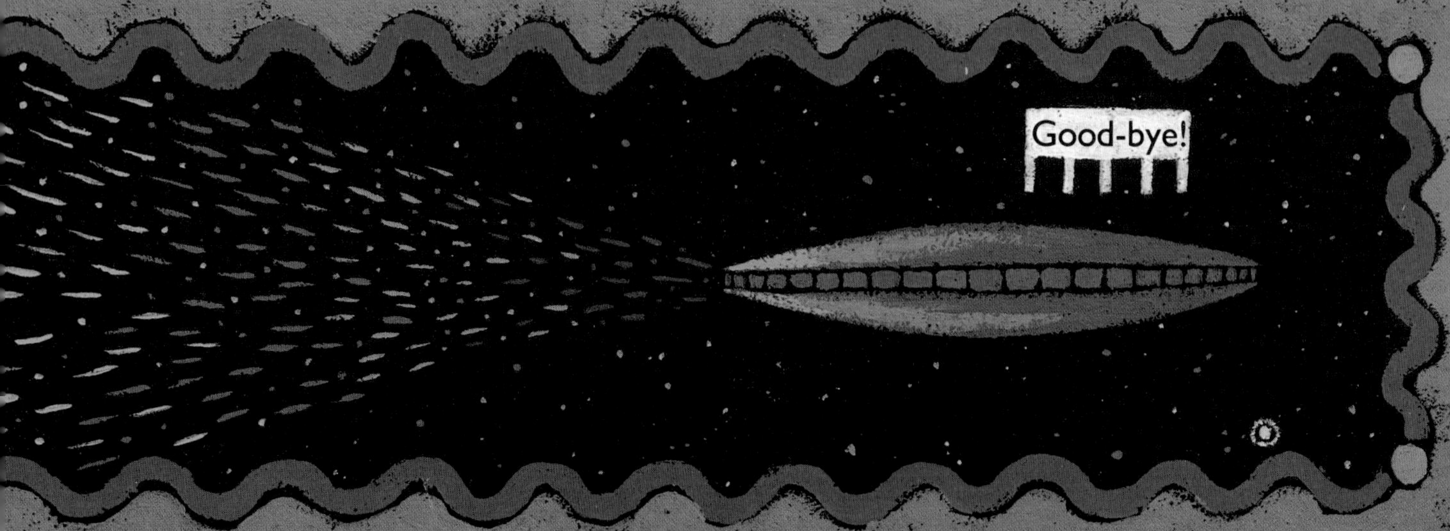
Good-bye!

OUR TRIP TO EARTH

THE GREAT WALL OF CHINA IN ASIA

THE PYRAMIDS IN AFRICA

REDWOOD FOREST IN NORTH AMERICA

INCAN RUINS IN SOUTH AMERICA

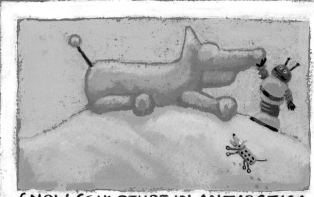

SNOW SCULPTURE IN ANTARCTICA

SKIING IN THE ALPS IN EUROPE

THE GREAT BARRIER REEF IN AUSTRALIA

THE EARTH—A BEAUTIFUL PLANET!